KUDO MARTIAL ARTS

Fundamentals And Methods Of Self-Defense: From Basics To Advanced Techniques

QIÁNG ZĬMÒ

Copyright © 2024 By Qiáng Zǐmò

All Rights Reserved

Table of Contents

Introductory 4

CHAPTER ONE 6

  Principles And Philosophy 6

  Basics Of Kudo Stances And Footwork .10

CHAPTER TWO 15

  Fundamentals Of Striking And Blocking 15

  Grappling And Ground Techniques 21

CHAPTER THREE 28

  Weapon Applications In Kudo 28

  Training Methods And Exercises 32

CHAPTER FOUR 38

  Strategies For Competitive Success......38

  Practical Self-Defense Techniques 43

  Summary..49

THE END 52

Introductory

Modern Japanese martial art Kudo was established in the 1980s. Takashi Azuma, desiring to create a practical and effective combat sport that fused elements of traditional martial arts such as karate, judo, and kickboxing, designed it.

Kudo martial arts integrate full-contact sparring while utilizing protective equipment such as gloves, headgear, and shin shields. The system prioritizes authentic combat situations and permits an extensive array of maneuvers, such as grappling, hurling, and striking. Kudo is a comprehensive martial art in that standing and ground combat are customary in competitions.

Kudo is distinguished by the implementation of a helmet design that permits headbutts, an action that is generally prohibited in combat sports. This incorporation exemplifies Kudo's emphasis on pragmatic methods of self-defense.

In general, Kudo endeavors to cultivate versatile martial practitioners well-versed in multiple facets of combat, rendering it applicable to both self-defense and competitive engagements.

CHAPTER ONE
Principles And Philosophy

The philosophy and guiding principles of Kudo are indicative of its prioritization of efficacy, practicality, and individual growth. The following are several pivotal components:

- The influence of Bushido: Kudo integrates components of traditional Japanese martial arts philosophy, specifically the tenets of self-discipline, loyalty, and honor that comprise the Bushido concept. These principles are to be embodied by practitioners both within and beyond the dojo.

- Practicality and Realism: Kudo prioritizes realistic combat scenarios and self-defense techniques that demonstrate efficacy in real-life situations. Sparring involving full contact and realistic scenarios are components of training that equip students for actual confrontations.

- Flexibility: Kudo does not adhere inflexibly to particular techniques or aesthetics. However, it promotes the idea that practitioners ought to modify and advance their methodologies in accordance with their unique aptitudes, limitations, and the circumstances at hand.

- Holistic Development: Kudo fosters mental and spiritual development in addition to physical prowess. Frequently incorporated into training sessions are philosophical discourse, breathing exercises, and meditation—all with the intention of cultivating self-awareness, mental fortitude, and emotional equilibrium.

• Discipline and Respect Kudo, similar to numerous martial arts, instills a profound sense of esteem for instructors, training companions, and adversaries. It is expected that practitioners exhibit qualities of discipline, humility, and courtesy in their conduct beyond the mat.

• Kudo incorporates the Kaizen philosophy, which stands for continuous improvement. It is recommended that practitioners consistently hone their abilities, broaden their understanding, and endeavor towards self-improvement.

• Self-Defense Orientation: Although Kudo does provide opportunities for competition, its fundamental emphasis continues to be on pragmatic self-defense. Techniques are selected and improved in accordance with their efficacy in practical conflicts, as opposed to being developed exclusively for athletic objectives.

• Unity of Mind and Body: Kudo endeavors to foster in its practitioners the unity of intellect, physique, and spirit. By engaging in spiritual investigation, physical training, and mental discipline, practitioners strive to attain equilibrium and harmony in every facet of their lives.

In addition to physical prowess, the philosophy and principles of Kudo foster inmates' personal development, ethical behavior, and a more profound comprehension of others.

Basics Of Kudo Stances And Footwork

In Kudo, stances and footwork are fundamental components that contribute to balance, mobility, and effective technique execution. Here are some basics:

• **Natural Stance**: The natural stance in Kudo is a balanced and relaxed posture with feet shoulder-width apart. Knees are slightly bent, and the body is centered and upright. This stance allows for quick movement in any direction and facilitates stability and readiness to engage or defend.

• **Forward Stance (Zenkutsu-dachi)**: The forward stance is commonly used in Kudo for attacking and advancing. In this stance, one leg is extended forward with the knee bent, while the other leg is positioned behind for support. The weight is distributed evenly between both legs, providing stability and power generation for strikes.

• **Backward Stance (Kokutsu-dachi)**: The backward stance is utilized for retreating or defending against incoming attacks. In this stance, one leg is stepped back behind the body while the front leg maintains a bent knee position. The weight is shifted slightly backward, allowing for quick evasion or counterattacks.

• **Side Stance (Kiba-dachi)**: The side stance is employed in Kudo for lateral movement and evasive maneuvers. In this stance, both feet are parallel and shoulder-width apart, with knees bent and weight evenly distributed. The body is turned slightly to the side, presenting a smaller target to the opponent while maintaining mobility.

• **Footwork**: Footwork in Kudo emphasizes agility, balance, and efficient movement. Practitioners learn various stepping patterns and techniques to navigate the combat space effectively, close the distance to attack, or create distance to evade and counter. Common footwork drills include stepping forward, backward, sideways, and pivoting to angle off or circle around opponents.

• **Shifts and Turns**: Kudo incorporates shifts and turns to enhance agility and create openings for attacks or defenses. Shifting involves transferring weight from one foot to the other to change direction or adjust positioning, while turning involves rotating the body to face a different direction or angle relative to the opponent.

• **Dynamic Balance**: Throughout stances and footwork, maintaining dynamic balance is crucial in Kudo.

Practitioners strive to stay grounded and centered while moving, striking, or defending, ensuring stability and readiness to respond to changing situations effectively.

By mastering stances and footwork fundamentals, Kudo practitioners develop the foundation for executing techniques with precision, fluidity, and effectiveness in both training and real-world combat scenarios.

CHAPTER TWO
Fundamentals Of Striking And Blocking

In Kudo, striking and blocking are essential components of combat, focusing on both offensive and defensive capabilities. Here are the fundamentals of striking and blocking in Kudo:

Striking Techniques:

• **Jabs (Tsuki)**: Straight punches aimed at the opponent's face or body using the lead hand.

• **Crosses (Gyaku Tsuki)**: Powerful punches thrown with the rear hand, often following a jab or setup.

- **Hooks (Kagi Tsuki)**: Circular punches delivered with a bent arm, targeting the opponent's head or body from the side.

- **Uppercuts (Shita Tsuki)**: Punches thrown upward from a low position, usually aiming for the chin or solar plexus.

- **Kicks (Geri)**: Various kicking techniques such as front kicks, roundhouse kicks, side kicks, and spinning kicks aimed at different targets like the legs, body, or head.

- **Knee Strikes (Hiza)**: Strikes using the knee, typically directed at the opponent's midsection or thighs in close-range combat.

- **Elbows (Empi)**: Strikes using the elbow, employed in short-range combat to deliver powerful blows to the opponent's face or body.

Blocking Techniques:

- **High Blocks (Jodan Uke)**: Defenses against attacks aimed at the head or upper body using the forearms or elbows to intercept or redirect incoming strikes.

- **Middle Blocks (Chudan Uke)**: Blocks used to defend against midsection attacks, often executed with the arms or elbows to absorb or deflect strikes.

- **Low Blocks (Gedan Barai)**: Defenses against kicks or low strikes directed at the legs or lower body, employing the arms or legs to intercept or deflect incoming attacks.

- **Parries (Uchi Uke)**: Redirecting incoming strikes by using the arms or hands to deflect the opponent's limb away from its intended target.

- **Evading (Tai Sabaki)**: Moving the body out of the path of incoming strikes through stepping, shifting, or pivoting to avoid contact altogether.

- **Combination Techniques**: Kudo practitioners often train to chain together multiple strikes and blocks fluidly to create effective combinations. Combinations may involve transitioning between different types of strikes and blocks to maintain pressure on the opponent and exploit openings in their defense.

• **Timing and Distance**: Mastery of striking and blocking in Kudo requires understanding proper timing and distance management. Practitioners learn to gauge the appropriate moment to launch attacks or defend against incoming strikes based on the opponent's movements and positioning.

• **Drills and Sparring**: Training in Kudo involves repetitive drills to develop muscle memory and refine striking and blocking techniques. Additionally, sparring sessions allow practitioners to test their skills in realistic combat scenarios, honing their ability to apply techniques under pressure while also sharpening their defensive instincts and reactions.

By mastering the fundamentals of striking and blocking in Kudo, practitioners develop the capability to effectively engage in combat, whether in training, competition, or self-defense situations.

Grappling And Ground Techniques

In Kudo, grappling and ground techniques are crucial components that complement striking and provide practitioners with a well-rounded skill set for close-quarters combat. Here are some fundamental grappling and ground techniques in Kudo:

Throws (Nage Waza):

• **Hip Throw (O-Goshi)**: A powerful throw where the practitioner uses their hip to lift and project the opponent over their shoulder and onto the ground.

• **Shoulder Throw (Seoi-Nage)**: A throwing technique where the practitioner grips the opponent's upper body and rotates, using their shoulder as a fulcrum to throw them over their back.

• **Leg Sweep (Deashi Harai)**: A sweeping motion aimed at the opponent's legs to disrupt their balance and bring them to the ground.

• **Inner Thigh Throw (Uchi-Mata)**: A throw where the practitioner hooks their leg around the opponent's thigh and lifts, using their hip to throw them off balance and onto the ground.

Joint Locks (Kansetsu Waza):

• **Arm Locks (Ude Garami)**: Techniques that involve manipulating the opponent's arm joints, such as the elbow or wrist, to apply pressure and control their movement.

- **Leg Locks (Ashi Gatame)**: Locking techniques targeting the opponent's legs, ankles, or knees to immobilize or submit them.

- **Wrist Locks (Kote Gaeshi)**: Techniques that involve twisting or bending the opponent's wrist joint to create pain compliance or control.

Chokes and Strangles (Shime Waza):

- **Rear Naked Choke (Hadaka Jime)**: A chokehold applied from the rear, where the practitioner wraps their arm around the opponent's neck and applies pressure to restrict blood flow to the brain.

- **Guillotine Choke (Mae Hadaka Jime)**: A chokehold applied from the front, where the practitioner traps the opponent's head under their arm and applies pressure to the neck.

- **Triangle Choke (Sankaku Jime)**: A submission hold where the practitioner traps the opponent's head and arm using their legs, creating a triangular configuration to apply pressure to the opponent's neck and arteries.

Ground Control and Positioning:

- **Mount Position (Tate Shiho Gatame)**: A dominant ground position where the practitioner straddles the opponent's torso, pinning them to the ground while maintaining balance and control.

• **Side Control (Yoko Shiho Gatame)**: Another dominant ground position where the practitioner lies perpendicular to the opponent, controlling their upper body and restricting movement.

• **Guard (Tate Shizen)**: A defensive position where the practitioner is on their back, using their legs and arms to control the opponent and prevent them from advancing or striking.

• **Transitions and Escapes**: Practitioners in Kudo train to smoothly transition between various grappling positions and techniques, as well as to escape from disadvantageous positions on the ground. This includes techniques such as bridging, shrimping, and hip escapes to create space and regain control.

• **Submission Holds and Escapes**: Kudo practitioners learn to apply a variety of submission holds to force opponents to submit or tap out. They also train in techniques to escape from submission attempts, such as counters, reversals, and proper defensive positioning.

By mastering grappling and ground techniques in Kudo, practitioners gain the ability to control and neutralize opponents in close-quarters combat, whether standing or on the ground, making them well-prepared for a wide range of self-defense scenarios or competitive engagements.

CHAPTER THREE
Weapon Applications In Kudo

In Kudo, although the primary focus is on unarmed combat, practitioners may also train in weapon applications for self-defense and traditional martial arts training purposes. Here are some common weapon applications in Kudo:

- **Bo (Staff)**: The staff is a versatile weapon commonly used in traditional martial arts. In Kudo, practitioners may learn techniques for striking, blocking, and disarming opponents using a staff. Training with the staff helps develop coordination, timing, and spatial awareness.

- **Bokken (Wooden Sword)**: The bokken, or wooden sword, is used in

Kudo to practice sword techniques derived from Japanese kenjutsu and kendo. Practitioners learn forms and drills for striking, blocking, and countering with the bokken, simulating combat scenarios while emphasizing control and precision.

• **Tanto (Knife)**: Knife defense is an essential aspect of self-defense training in Kudo. Practitioners learn techniques to defend against knife attacks, including disarms, blocks, and evasions. Training in knife defense helps develop awareness, reflexes, and effective responses to close-range threats.

• **Nunchaku (Nunchucks)**: The nunchaku is a traditional Okinawan weapon consisting of two sticks connected by a chain or rope. In Kudo, practitioners may train with the nunchaku to develop coordination, speed, and fluidity of movement. Techniques include striking, blocking, and trapping opponents' limbs.

- **Tonfa**: The tonfa is a martial arts weapon originating from Okinawa, consisting of a stick with a handle perpendicular to the length of the shaft. In Kudo, practitioners may learn tonfa techniques for striking, blocking, and controlling opponents, often emphasizing close-range combat and joint manipulation.

- **Kubotan**: The kubotan is a small, handheld self-defense tool used for striking vulnerable points on an attacker's body. In Kudo, practitioners may train in kubotan techniques for self-defense purposes, focusing on pressure point strikes, joint locks, and control holds.

• **Improvised Weapons**: In addition to traditional martial arts weapons, Kudo practitioners may train in using everyday objects as improvised weapons for self-defense. Techniques include utilizing items such as keys, pens, or umbrellas to strike, block, or disarm attackers in close-quarters combat situations.

While the emphasis in Kudo remains on unarmed combat and self-defense techniques applicable in real-world scenarios, training in weapon applications provides practitioners with additional skills, versatility, and understanding of martial arts principles and concepts. Moreover, it fosters a deeper appreciation for traditional martial arts culture and heritage.

Training Methods And Exercises

In Kudo, a variety of training methods and exercises are employed to develop a well-rounded martial artist with skills in striking, grappling, ground fighting, and self-defense. Here are some common training methods and exercises used in Kudo:

- **Basic Techniques Drills**: Practitioners often start with drills focused on fundamental techniques such as punches, kicks, blocks, and stances. These drills help develop proper form, timing, and coordination.

• **Pad Work**: Pad work involves striking focus mitts, kicking shields, or heavy bags held by a training partner or instructor. This training method allows practitioners to practice their strikes with resistance and feedback, enhancing power, speed, and accuracy.

• **Partner Drills**: Partner drills involve practicing techniques with a training partner in a controlled and cooperative environment. This includes practicing striking combinations, blocking and countering drills, and practicing throws and takedowns.

- **Sparring**: Sparring sessions allow practitioners to apply techniques learned in training in a dynamic and realistic setting. Depending on the level of intensity, sparring can range from light, technical sparring to full-contact matches. Sparring helps practitioners develop timing, distance management, and decision-making under pressure.

- **Ground Fighting Drills**: Ground fighting drills focus on techniques for grappling, submissions, and ground control. This includes practicing transitions between positions, escapes from submissions, and submissions themselves.

- **Conditioning Training**: Conditioning exercises such as running, calisthenics, and strength training are essential for developing physical fitness and endurance. This includes exercises to improve cardiovascular fitness, muscular strength, and flexibility.

• **Functional Training**: Functional training involves exercises that mimic movements and muscle actions used in martial arts techniques. This can include exercises such as medicine ball throws, kettlebell swings, and agility drills to improve explosive power, agility, and coordination.

• **Kata and Forms Practice**: Kata, or forms, are pre-arranged sequences of movements that simulate combat scenarios against imaginary opponents. Practicing kata helps practitioners develop muscle memory, focus, and understanding of martial arts principles.

• **Visualization and Mental Training**: Mental training techniques such as visualization, meditation, and breathing exercises are used to develop focus, concentration, and mental resilience. Visualization involves mentally rehearsing techniques and scenarios to enhance performance and confidence.

• **Scenario-based Training**: Scenario-based training involves simulating real-world self-defense situations to practice applying techniques under stress. This can include scenarios such as defending against multiple attackers, dealing with armed assailants, or responding to surprise attacks.

By incorporating a combination of these training methods and exercises, Kudo practitioners develop a comprehensive skill set encompassing striking, grappling, ground fighting, and self-defense, as well as physical fitness, mental toughness, and resilience. Additionally, training in Kudo fosters discipline, humility, and respect for oneself and others, contributing to personal growth and character development.

CHAPTER FOUR
Strategies For Competitive Success

Achieving success in competitive Kudo requires a combination of physical skill, mental fortitude, strategic thinking, and effective training. Here are some strategies that can help practitioners excel in Kudo competitions:

• **Master the Basics**: Focus on mastering fundamental techniques such as striking, grappling, throwing, and ground fighting. Solid proficiency in the basics forms the foundation for more advanced skills and strategies.

• **Train with Intensity**: Kudo competitions can be physically demanding and mentally challenging. Train with intensity and purpose to build stamina, strength, speed, and agility. Include drills and sparring sessions that simulate the pace and intensity of competition.

• **Develop Versatility**: Kudo encompasses a wide range of techniques from different martial arts disciplines. Develop proficiency in both striking and grappling to become a well-rounded martial artist capable of adapting to various opponents and situations.

• **Study Opponents**: Analyze opponents' strengths, weaknesses, and tendencies by watching their matches and studying their techniques. Identify patterns and develop strategies to exploit vulnerabilities while capitalizing on your own strengths.

• **Stay Calm Under Pressure**: Maintain composure and focus during matches, even in high-pressure situations. Practice relaxation techniques such as controlled breathing and visualization to manage nerves and maintain clarity of thought.

• **Exploit Openings**: Look for openings and opportunities to score points or secure submissions. Develop the ability to read opponents' movements and anticipate their actions to capitalize on openings effectively.

• **Adapt to the Ruleset**: Familiarize yourself with the rules and scoring criteria of Kudo competitions. Adjust your strategies and tactics accordingly to maximize scoring opportunities within the ruleset.

• **Condition Mentally and Emotionally**: Mental toughness is crucial in competitive Kudo. Develop resilience to setbacks, maintain a positive mindset, and learn from both victories and defeats to continually improve.

• **Work on Timing and Distance**: Master timing and distance management to control the pace of the match and dictate the engagement. Develop the ability to close the distance for attacks while avoiding opponents' strikes or takedowns.

- **Continuously Improve**: Embrace a growth mindset and continually seek ways to improve your skills and performance. Regularly evaluate your strengths and weaknesses, set goals, and strive for constant progress through focused training and deliberate practice.

By implementing these strategies and committing to consistent training and improvement, practitioners can increase their chances of achieving competitive success in Kudo tournaments and matches.

Practical Self-Defense Techniques

Practical self-defense techniques in Kudo are designed to be effective in real-life situations where individuals may need to defend themselves against physical attacks. These techniques focus on simplicity, efficiency, and adaptability. Here are some common self-defense techniques practiced in Kudo:

• **Awareness and Avoidance**: The first line of self-defense is awareness of your surroundings and potential threats. Avoid potentially dangerous situations whenever possible by staying alert and trusting your instincts to recognize and avoid potential confrontations.

- **Verbal De-escalation**: Attempt to defuse confrontations verbally by using assertive yet non-aggressive communication. Remain calm, maintain eye contact, and speak confidently to assert boundaries and deter potential attackers.

Striking Techniques:

1. **Palm Strikes**: Use the palm of your hand to strike vulnerable areas such as the nose, chin, or throat of an attacker.
2. **Elbow Strikes**: Employ elbow strikes to deliver powerful blows to the attacker's face, solar plexus, or ribs in close-range combat.

3. **Knee Strikes**: Use knee strikes to target the attacker's groin, abdomen, or thighs when in close proximity.

• **Blocking and Deflecting**: Practice blocking and deflecting incoming strikes to minimize the impact of attacks. Techniques such as forearm blocks, parries, and evasion can help create openings for counterattacks or create distance to escape.

Grappling and Joint Manipulation:

1. **Joint Locks**: Apply joint locks to control and immobilize the attacker's limbs, such as wrist locks, elbow locks, or shoulder locks.

2. **Escapes**: Learn techniques to escape from grabs, holds, or grappling situations, including wrist releases, arm bars, or hip escapes.

Ground Defense:

1. **Guard Position**: If taken to the ground, assume a defensive guard position to protect vital areas and create opportunities for escape or counterattacks.
2. **Ground Strikes**: Utilize strikes from the ground, such as hammer fists or kicks, to fend off attackers and create openings for standing up or escaping.

Escape Techniques:

1. **Escape from Holds**: Practice techniques to escape from common holds such as wrist grabs, bear hugs, or chokeholds.
2. **Strategic Retreat**: When facing multiple attackers or overwhelming odds, prioritize escape and evasion over engaging in prolonged combat.
3. **Weapons Defense**: If faced with an armed attacker, focus on disarming techniques and creating distance to neutralize the threat. Utilize improvised weapons if available and prioritize survival.

- **Scenario-based Training**: Train in simulated self-defense scenarios to practice applying techniques under pressure and develop confidence in your ability to defend yourself effectively in real-life situations.

- **Legal and Ethical Considerations**: Understand the legal and ethical implications of self-defense actions in your jurisdiction. Use only the necessary level of force to protect yourself or others and prioritize de-escalation and escape whenever possible.

Through diligent training and attainment of proficiency in these pragmatic self-defense strategies within the realm of Kudo, individuals can bolster their capacity to shield themselves and others from perilous circumstances, thereby advancing their own security and welfare.

Summary

Kudo, an all-encompassing martial art, integrates components of ground combat, striking, grappling, and self-defense methodologies. Kudo places significant emphasis on pragmatic and efficient approaches, prioritizing versatile strategies and realistic combat scenarios that can be applied in both competitive and self-defense contexts.

Kudo training methods and techniques foster not only physical prowess but also psychological fortitude, emotional equilibrium, and individual development. Through the acquisition of proficiency in the foundational principles of Kudo, adherents cultivate self-assurance and the capacity to safeguard oneself, all the while promoting discipline, esteem, and companionship among members of the martial arts community.

Kudo, a contemporary martial art with roots in Japan and an extensive international following, has undergone continuous development and flourished as a means of empowering individuals to safeguard themselves, improve their physical well-being, and foster a more profound comprehension of martial arts principles and philosophies.

Pupils of Kudo exemplify the essence of Bushido, whether they are engaged in self-defense, competitive training, or personal growth. In their pursuit of martial excellence, they exhibit both skill and integrity. Proficients of Kudo establish a trajectory of fortitude, self-realization, and fortitude that transcends the boundaries of the dojo by means of diligence, perseverance, and an unwavering dedication to enhancement.

THE END

Made in the USA
Monee, IL
20 April 2024